C000138557

I love you Mom...

I love you
Mom...

and all the things you say and do

Susan Akass

illustrations by Hannah George

CICO BOOKS
LONDON NEW YORK

Published in 2011 by CICO Books
An imprint of Ryland Peters & Small
519 Broadway, 5th Floor,
New York NY 10012
20–21 Jockey's Fields,
London WC1R 4BW

www.cicobooks.com

10 9 8 7 6 5 4 3 2

Text © Susan Akass 2011
Design and illustration © CICO Books 2011

A CIP catalog record for this
book is available from the Library
of Congress and the British Library.

US ISBN: 978 1 907563 27 0

UK ISBN: 978 1 907563 11 9

Printed in China

Design: David Fordham
Illustration: Hannah George

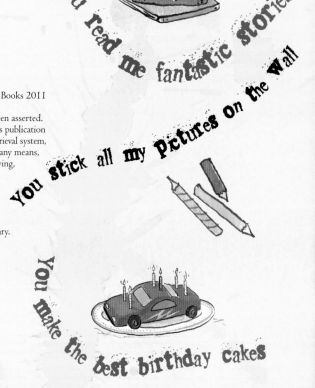

You read me fantastic stories

You stick all my pictures on the wall

You make the best birthday cakes

I love you,
because...

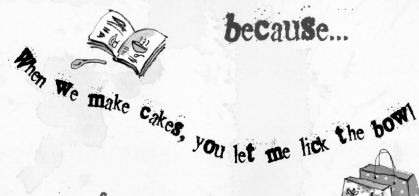

When we make cakes, you let me lick the bowl

We have fun when we go shopping together

You helped me build the biggest snowman

You plait my hair
for parties

When

I build a den

in the garden,

you bring me

food supplies

You dug me a garden and
I grew my OWN carrots
and strawberries

When we make cakes, you let me *lick* the bowl

You're not CROSS
When I make
mistakes

You're a **FANTASTIC** cook –your roast dinners are **AMAZING**

You dance round the kitchen to the music you love

You helped me to **CATCH** my hamster

when it **ESCAPED**

We both enjoy
M^ESS_ING
around with paints
and paper and glue

You organize
GREAT
barbecues for all
our friends and
family

When it is hot you
fill up
the **paddling pool**
and squirt

me with the hose

squirt
squirt

Wherever We go you bring a bag
full of **APPLES** and **COOKIES**
and **DRINKS** and **TISSUES**

You made me a
BRILLIANT costume
for the school play

You invited my
friends for a
sleepover
and helped us
paint our nails

You knit me SWEATERS that are TOO BIG for me and they keep me all snugly and warm

You pick me
up and kiss me
better
When I'm hurt

We play
hospitals and
you let me
bandage you up

You make bath time FUN with toys and bubbles and Waterfalls

You stick ALL
my pictures on the
WALL

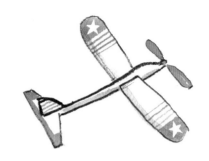

You bought me an **ENORMOUS** SUPER SOAKER WATER BLASTER for my last birthday

You decorated my room and let ME choose the paint

We SNUGGLE on
the sofa and you cry
over my girly
DVDs

You help me with my reading
and test me on my spelling

You taught
me to tie my shoelaces

When my sports gear
is MUDDY,
you get it CLEAN

You try to play **soccer** and once you made an **AWESOME** Save

We play LOTS
of games and
I beat you at
SNAP!

You make the

BEST

BIRTHDAY CAKES

You took me fishing for TADPOLES and we kept them till they changed into FROGS

When I lose **things**
you **ALWAYS**
know **where to look**

You read me

FANTASTIC stories

again and again and again

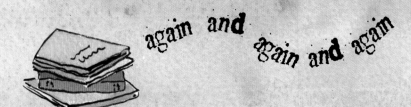

again and again and again

again and again and again

You

scREAMED

When there was a

spider

and I had to catch it

You make sure the
cupboards

are always full of
yummy food

We have **FUN** When
We go shopping
together

You helped me build the biggest snowman

When you go out,
you KISS me
goodnight and always
look BEAUTIFUL and

SMELL of LOVELY

perfume

You're the BEST!

I love you because...

1 ....

2 ....

3 ....

4 ....

5 ....